Vintage Flowers
Coloring

new seasons®
a division of Publications International, Ltd.

Let's get social!

 @Publications_International

 @PublicationsInternational

www.pilbooks.com

Earth laughs in flowers.

— Ralph Waldo Emerson, Hamatreya

We gathered the wild-flowers.
Yes, life there seem'd one pure delight;
As thro' the field we rov'd.
Yes, life there seem'd one pure delight.

—George Linley

A garden is evidence of faith. It links us with all
the misty figures of the past who also planted and
were nourished by the fruits of their planting.

—Gladys Taber

When in these fresh mornings I go into my garden before anyone is awake, I go for the time being into perfect happiness. In this hour divinely fresh and still, the fair face of every flower salutes me with a silent joy.

—Celia Thaxter

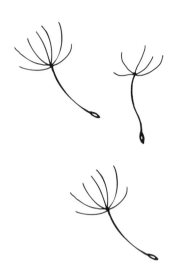

O dandelion, rich and haughty,
King of village flowers!
Each day is coronation time,
You have no humble hours.
I like to see you bring a troop
To beat the blue-grass spears,
To scorn the lawn-mower that would be
Like fate's triumphant shears.
Your yellow heads are cut away,
It seems your reign is o'er.
By noon you raise a sea of stars
More golden than before.

—Vachel Lindsay, The Dandelion

Every flower is a soul blossoming in nature.

—Gérard de Nerval

A garden that one makes oneself becomes
associated with one's personal history and that of
one's friends, interwoven with one's tastes,
preferences and character, and constitutes a sort
of unwritten, but withal manifest, autobiography.
Show me your garden, provided it be your own,
and I will tell you what you are like.

—Alfred Austin

A red rose is not selfish because it wants
to be a red rose. It would be horribly
selfish if it wanted all the other flowers in
the garden to be both red and roses.

—Oscar Wilde

In the hope of reaching the moon men fail to see
the flowers that blossom at their feet.

—Albert Schweitzer

If seeds in the black earth can turn into such beautiful roses, what might not the heart of man become in its long journey toward the stars?

—G.K. Chesterton

How does the Meadow-flower its bloom unfold?
Because the lovely little flower is free
Down to its root, and, in that freedom, bold.

—William Wordsworth,
A Poet! He Hath Put his Heart to School

Flowers are love's truest language.

—Park Benjamin

Won't you come into the garden?
I would like my roses to see you.

—Richard Brinsley Sheridan

He who is born with a silver spoon in his mouth is generally considered a fortunate person, but his good fortune is small compared to that of the happy mortal who enters this world with a passion for flowers in his soul.

—Celia Thaxter

As well as any bloom upon a flower
I like the dust on the nettles, never lost
Except to prove the sweetness of a shower.

—Edward Thomas, Tall Nettles

I will be the gladdest thing
under the sun!
I will touch a hundred flowers
And not pick one.

—Edna St. Vincent Millay, Afternoon on a Hill

All my hurts my garden spade can heal.

—Ralph Waldo Emerson

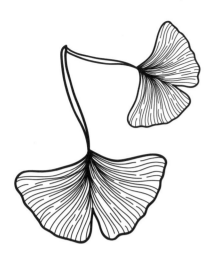

Even the scarlet flowers of passion seem to grow in
the same meadow as the poppies of oblivion.

—Oscar Wilde

Nature's first green is gold,
Her hardest hue to hold.
Her early leaf's a flower;
But only so an hour.

—Robert Frost, Nothing Gold Can Stay

If I had a flower for every time I thought of you...
I could walk through my garden forever.

—Alfred Tennyson

To analyze the charms of flowers is like dissecting music;
it is one of those things which it is far better to enjoy,
than to attempt to fully understand.

—Henry T. Tuckerman

O happy Garden! loved for hours of sleep,
O quiet Garden! loved for waking hours,
For soft half-slumbers that did gently steep
Our spirits, carrying with them dreams of flowers.

—William Wordsworth, Farewell,
Thou Little Nook of Mountain Ground

Keep love in your heart. A life without it is like a
sunless garden when the flowers are dead.
The consciousness of loving and being loved brings a
warmth and a richness to life that nothing else can bring.

—Oscar Wilde

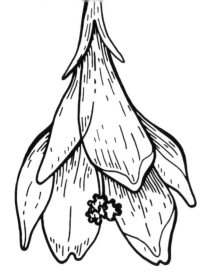

Shed no tear! O, shed no tear!
The flower will bloom another year.

—John Keats, Faery Songs

Let us be grateful to people who make us
happy, they are the charming gardeners
who make our souls blossom.

—Marcel Proust

In seed-time learn, in harvest teach, in winter enjoy.

— William Blake, The Marriage of Heaven and Hell

A gardening instinct, sore as the sap rising in the trees,
stirs within us. We look about and decide to tame
another little bit of ground.

— Lewis Gannett

What a desolate place would be a world without a flower! It would be a face without a smile, a feast without a welcome. Are not flowers the stars of the earth, and are not our stars the flowers of heaven?

—Clara Lucas Balfour

But now you love a hyacinth. So much the better.
You have gained a new source of enjoyment, and it is
well to have as many holds upon happiness as possible.

—Jane Austen, Northanger Abbey

So extraordinary is Nature with her choicest treasures, spending plant beauty as she spends sunshine, pouring it forth into land and sea, garden and desert. And so the beauty of lilies falls on angels and men, bears and squirrels, wolves and sheep, birds and bees...

— John Muir, My First Summer in the Sierra

A sensitive plant in a garden grew,
And the young winds fed it with silvery dew.

—Percy Bysshe Shelley, The Sensitive Plant

I perhaps owe having become a painter to flowers.

—Claude Monet

Flowers are beautiful hieroglyphics of Nature,
with which she indicates how much she loves us.

—Johann Wolfgang von Goethe

You love the roses — so do I. I wish
The sky would rain down roses, as they rain
From off the shaken bush. Why will it not?
Then all the valley would be pink and white
And soft to tread on. They would fall as light
As feathers, smelling sweet; and it would be
Like sleeping and like waking, all at once!

—George Eliot, Roses

To plant a garden is to dream of tomorrow.

— Audrey Hepburn

Through primrose tufts, in that green bower,
The periwinkle trailed its wreaths;
And 'tis my faith that every flower
Enjoys the air it breathes.

—William Wordsworth, Lines Written in Early Spring

You're only here for a short visit. Don't hurry, don't worry.
And be sure to smell the flowers along the way.

—Walter Hagen

I've always thought my flowers had souls.

—Myrtle Reed

In joy or sadness, flowers are our constant friends.
We eat, drink, sing, dance, and flirt with them. We wed
and christen with flowers. We dare not die without them.

— Kakuzo Okakura, The Book of Tea

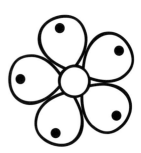

We don't ask a flower any special reason for its existence. We just look at it and are able to accept it as being something different for ourselves.

—Gwendolyn Brooks

Flowers... are a proud assertion that a ray of beauty outvalues all the utilities in the world.

—Ralph Waldo Emerson

The man who has planted a garden feels that he has done something for the good of the world.

—Charles Dudley Warner

The flower of sweetest smell is shy and lowly.

—William Wordsworth,
Not Love, Not War, Nor the Tumultuous Swell

The red rose whispers of passion,
And the white rose breathes of love;
O, the red rose is a falcon,
And the white rose is a dove.
But I send you a cream-white rosebud
With a flush on its petal tips;
For the love that is purest and sweetest
Has a kiss of desire on the lips.

—John Boyle O'Reilly, The White Rose

One of the most attractive things about the
flowers is their beautiful reserve.

—Henry David Thoreau

There is no gardening without humility, an assiduous willingness to learn and a cheerful readiness to confess you were mistaken. Nature is constantly sending even its oldest scholars to the bottom of the class for some egregious blunder.

—Alfred Austin

The meanest floweret of the vale,
The simplest note that swells the gale,
The common sun, the air, the skies,
To him are opening Paradise.

—Thomas Gray, Ode on the
Pleasure Arising from Vicissitude

Everybody needs beauty as well as bread,
places to play in and pray in, where nature may
heal and give strength to body and soul alike.

—John Muir, The Yosemite

The fairest flowers have cheered me with their sweet breath, fresh dew and fragrant leaves have been ever ready for me, gentle hands to tend, kindly hearts to love.

— Louisa May Alcott, Flower Fables

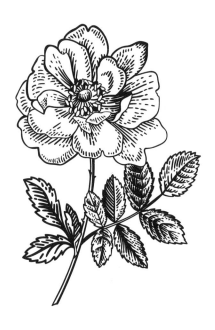

I'd rather have roses on my table
than diamonds on my neck.

—Emma Goldman

Many things grow in the garden
that were never sown there.

—Thomas Fuller

Ah Sun-flower! weary of time,
Who countest the steps of the Sun:
Seeking after that sweet golden clime
Where the travellers journey is done.

Where the Youth pined away with desire,
And the pale Virgin shrouded in snow:
Arise from their graves and aspire,
Where my Sun-flower wishes to go.

—William Blake, Ah! Sun-flower

A flowerless room is a soulless room, to my
way of thinking; but even one solitary little
vase of a living flower may redeem it.

—Vita Sackville-West

There is no time like the old time,
when you and I were young,
When the buds of April blossomed,
and the birds of spring-time sung!
The garden's brightest glories
by summer suns are nursed,
But oh, the sweet, sweet violets,
the flowers that opened first!

—Oliver Wendell Holmes,
No Time Like the Old Time

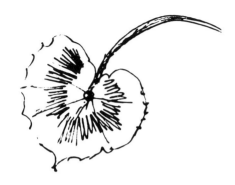

Good gardeners are always young in spirit,
for their minds are fixed on spring when
others feel only the bitter sting of winter.

—Mary Fanton Roberts

When you take a flower in your hand and really look at it,
it's your world for the moment. I want to give that world
to someone else. Most people in the city rush around
so, they have no time to look at a flower. I want them to
see it whether they want to or not.

—Georgia O'Keeffe

Flowers are words which even a baby can understand.

—A. Cleveland Coxe

I have a garden of my own,
But so with roses overgrown,
And lilies, that you would it guess
to be a little wilderness.

—Andrew Marvell, The Nymph Complaining
for the Death of her Fawn

Everything that slows us down and forces
patience, everything that sets us back into
the slow circles of nature is a help.
Gardening is an instrument of grace.

—May Sarton

Nothing seems worth doing but the laying out of gardens.

—Ralph Waldo Emerson

It is radiant in the sunshine, and so cheerful after rain;
And it wafts upon the air its sweet perfume.
It is very, very lovely! May its beauties never wane—
This dear flower at my window in full bloom.

— Lucian B. Watkins, The Flower at my Window

A flower blossoms for its own joy.

—Oscar Wilde

What I need most of all are flowers, always, always.

—Claude Monet